HOW TO [ ]
HALLOWEEN STUFF

THIS BOOK BELONGS TO:

_____

_____

STEP 6

STEP 5

STEP 4

STEP 3

STEP 2

STEP 1

NOW, IT'S YOUR TURN :)

STEP 6

STEP 5

STEP 4

STEP 3

STEP 2

STEP 1

NOW, IT'S YOUR TURN :)

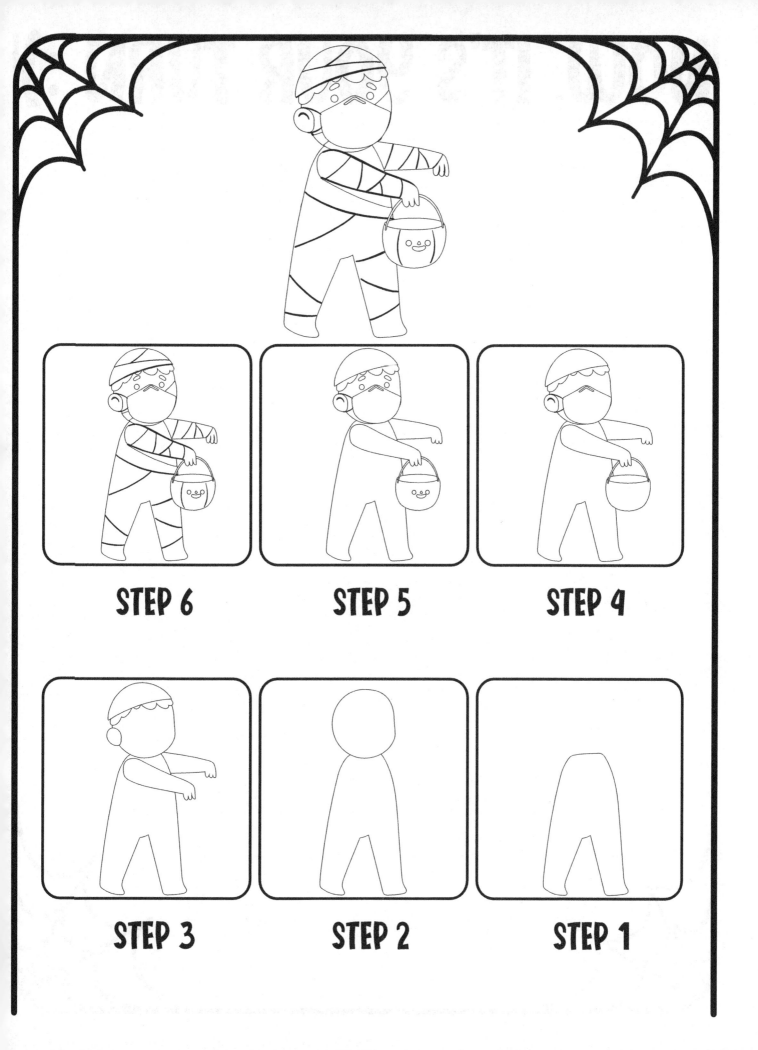

STEP 6

STEP 5

STEP 4

STEP 3

STEP 2

STEP 1

NOW, IT'S YOUR TURN :)

STEP 6

STEP 5

STEP 4

STEP 3

STEP 2

STEP 1

NOW, IT'S YOUR TURN :)

STEP 6

STEP 5

STEP 4

STEP 3

STEP 2

STEP 1

NOW, IT'S YOUR TURN :)

STEP 6

STEP 5

STEP 4

STEP 3

STEP 2

STEP 1

NOW, IT'S YOUR TURN :)

STEP 6

STEP 5

STEP 4

STEP 3

STEP 2

STEP 1

NOW, IT'S YOUR TURN :)

STEP 6

STEP 5

STEP 4

STEP 3

STEP 2

STEP 1

NOW, IT'S YOUR TURN :)

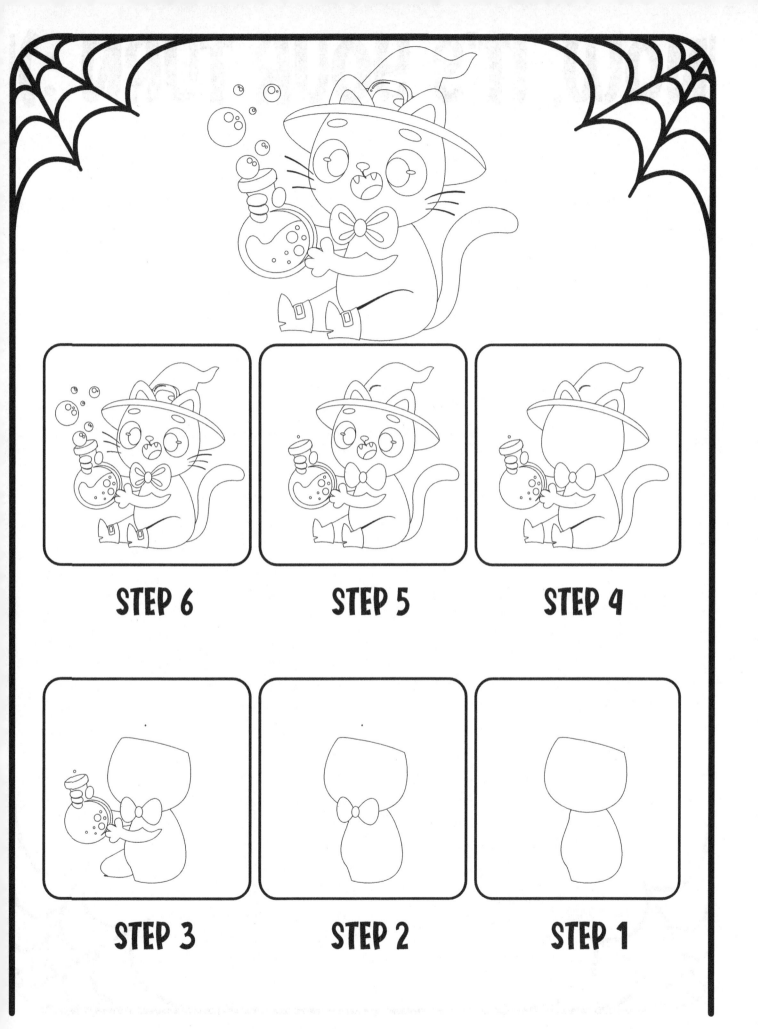

STEP 6

STEP 5

STEP 4

STEP 3

STEP 2

STEP 1

NOW, IT'S YOUR TURN :)

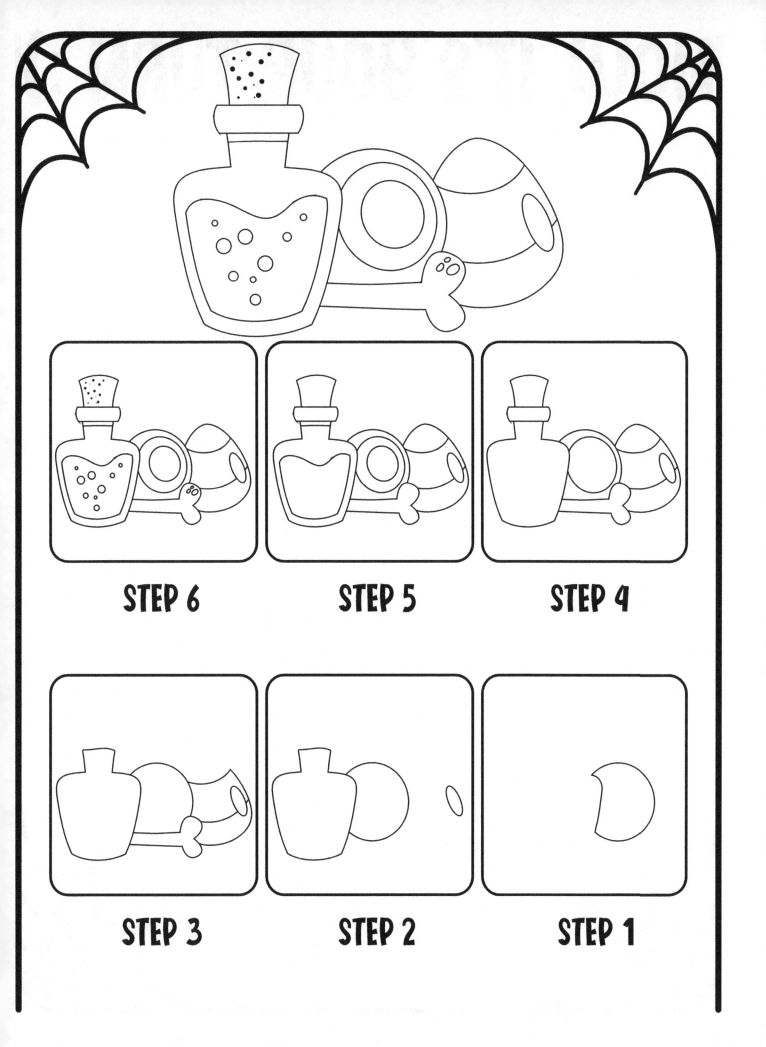

STEP 6

STEP 5

STEP 4

STEP 3

STEP 2

STEP 1

NOW, IT'S YOUR TURN :)

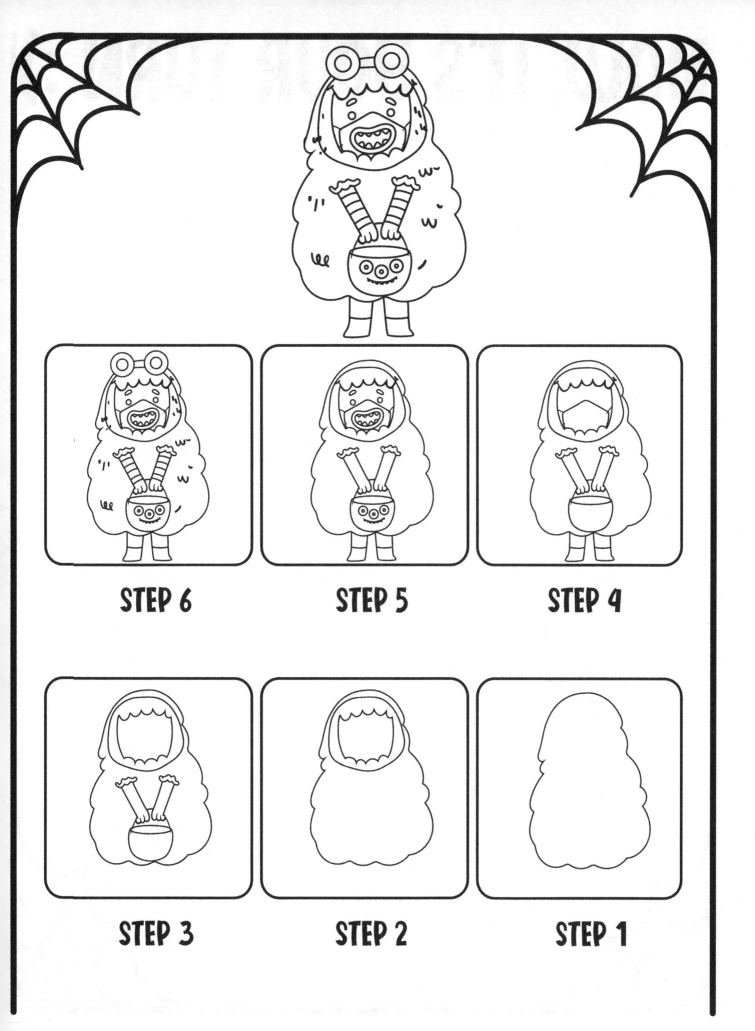

STEP 6

STEP 5

STEP 4

STEP 3

STEP 2

STEP 1

NOW, IT'S YOUR TURN :)

STEP 6

STEP 5

STEP 4

STEP 3

STEP 2

STEP 1

NOW, IT'S YOUR TURN :)

STEP 6

STEP 5

STEP 4

STEP 3

STEP 2

STEP 1

NOW, IT'S YOUR TURN :)

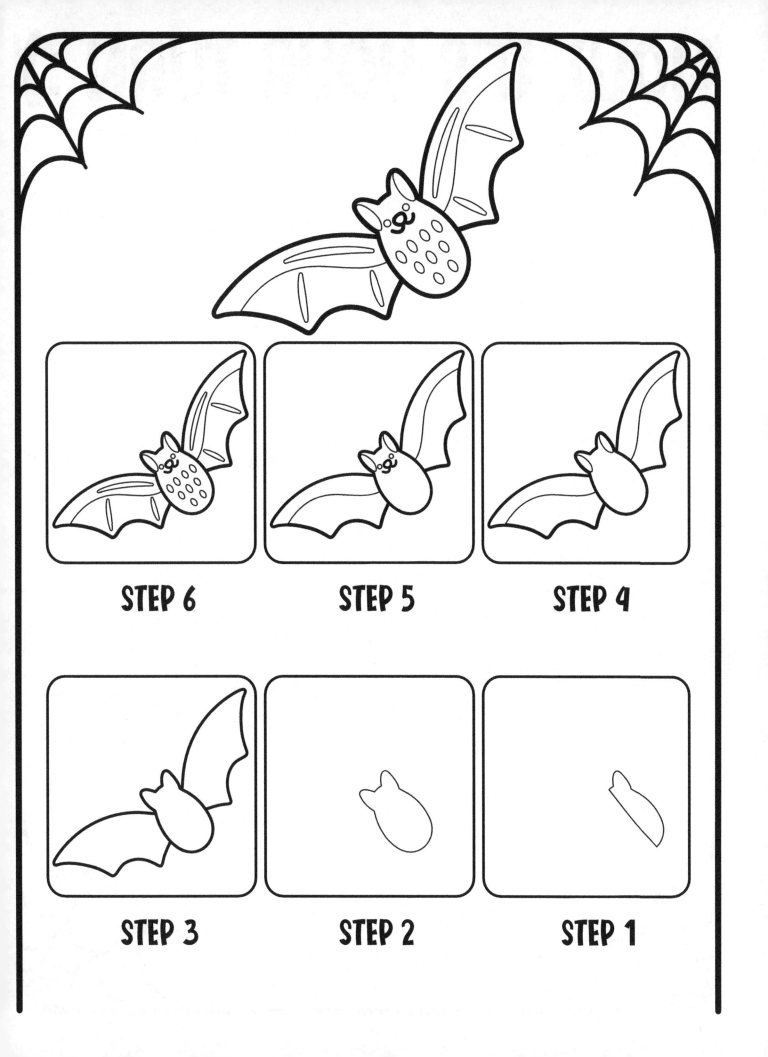

STEP 6

STEP 5

STEP 4

STEP 3

STEP 2

STEP 1

NOW, IT'S YOUR TURN :)

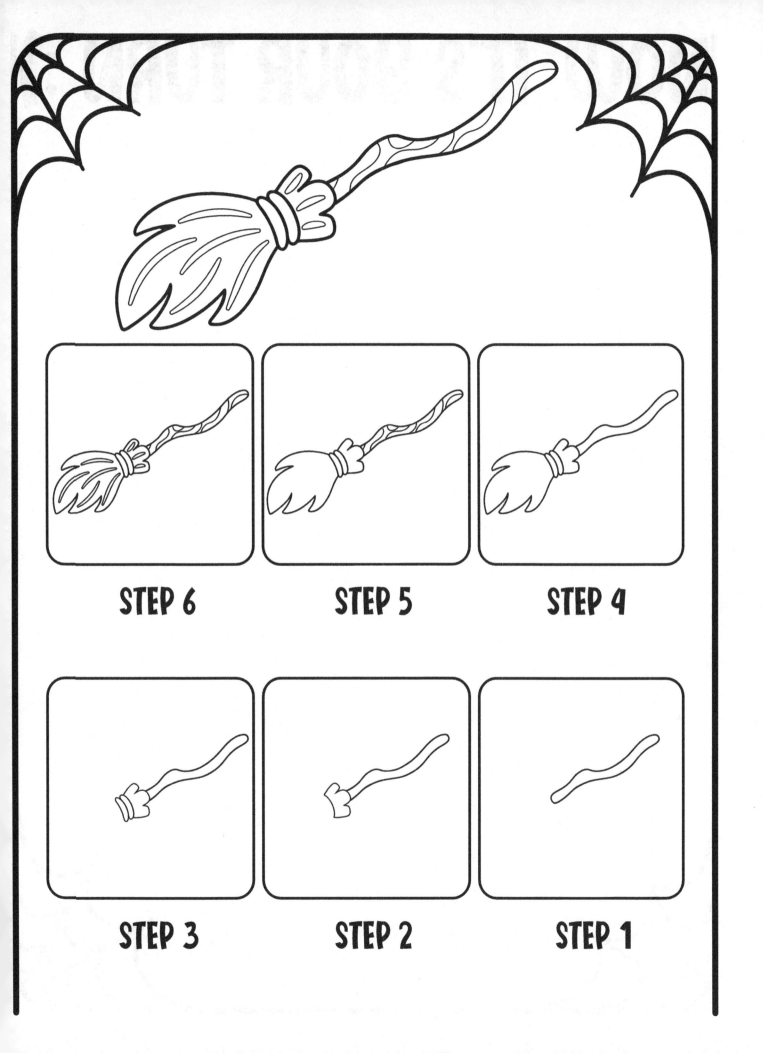

STEP 6

STEP 5

STEP 4

STEP 3

STEP 2

STEP 1

NOW, IT'S YOUR TURN :)

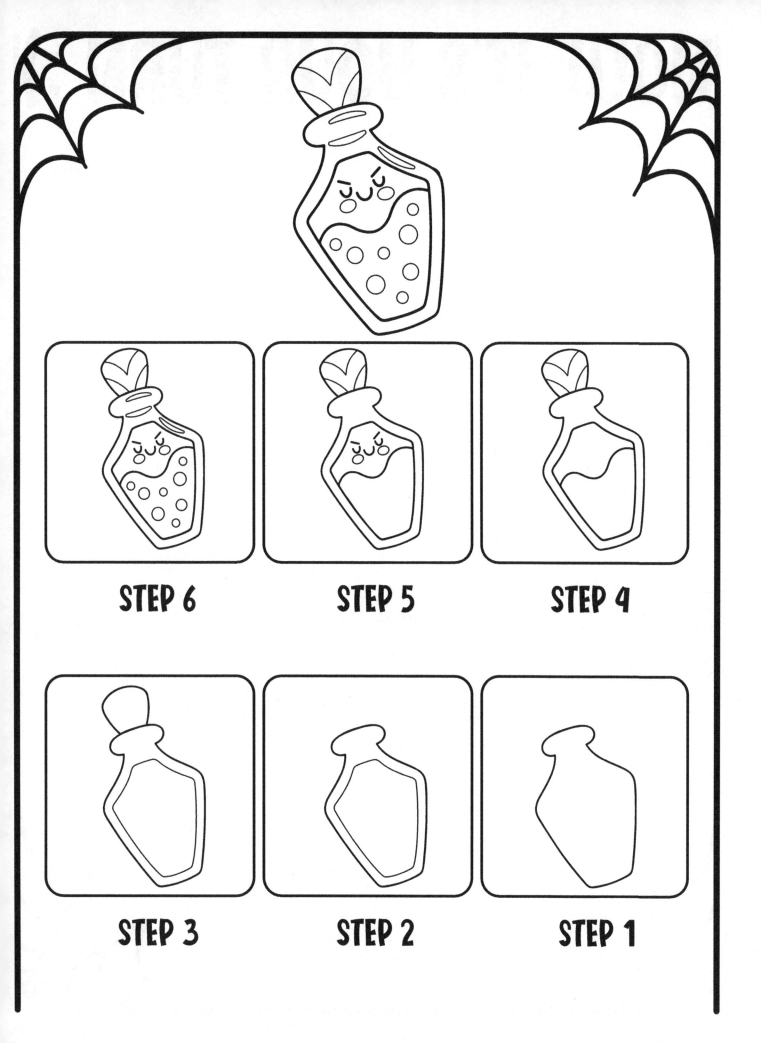

STEP 6

STEP 5

STEP 4

STEP 3

STEP 2

STEP 1

NOW, IT'S YOUR TURN :)

STEP 6

STEP 5

STEP 4

STEP 3

STEP 2

STEP 1

NOW, IT'S YOUR TURN :)

STEP 6

STEP 5

STEP 4

STEP 3

STEP 2

STEP 1

NOW, IT'S YOUR TURN :)

STEP 6

STEP 5

STEP 4

STEP 3

STEP 2

STEP 1

NOW, IT'S YOUR TURN :)

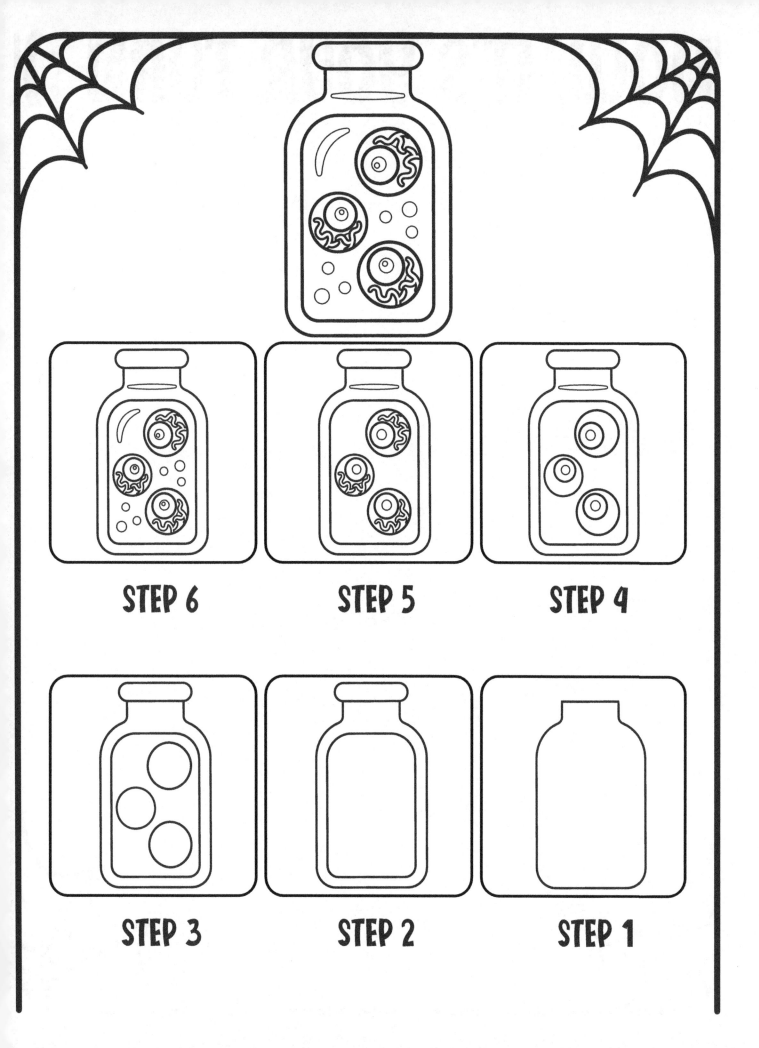

STEP 6

STEP 5

STEP 4

STEP 3

STEP 2

STEP 1

NOW, IT'S YOUR TURN :)

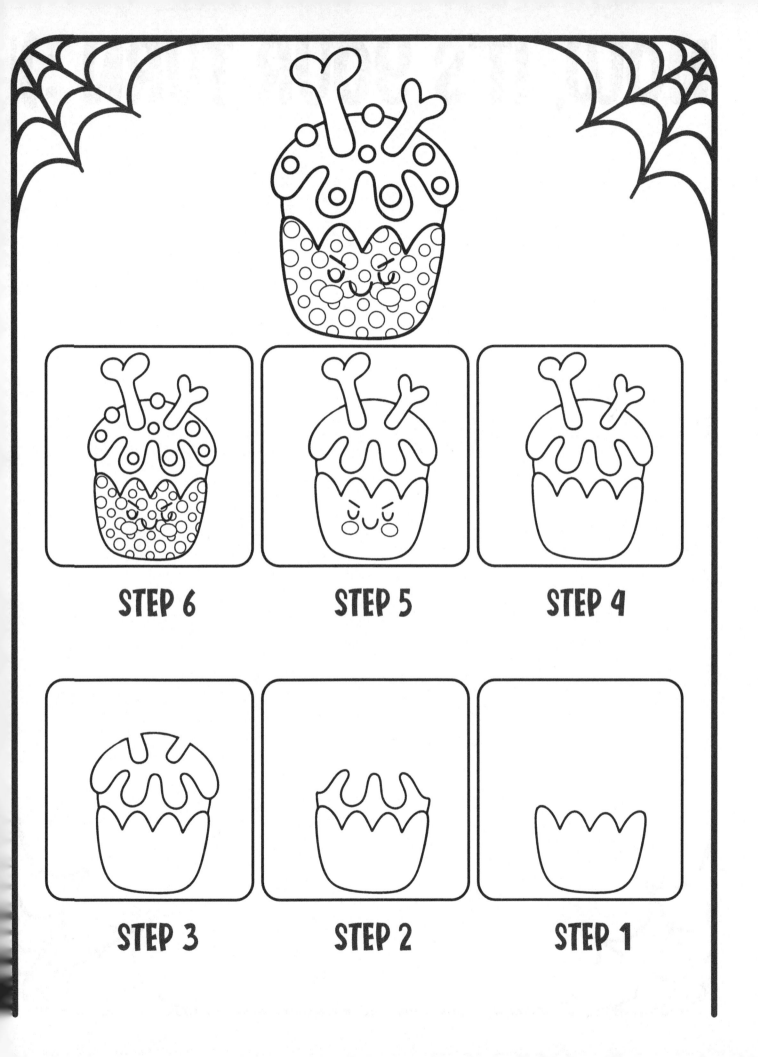

STEP 6

STEP 5

STEP 4

STEP 3

STEP 2

STEP 1

NOW, IT'S YOUR TURN :)

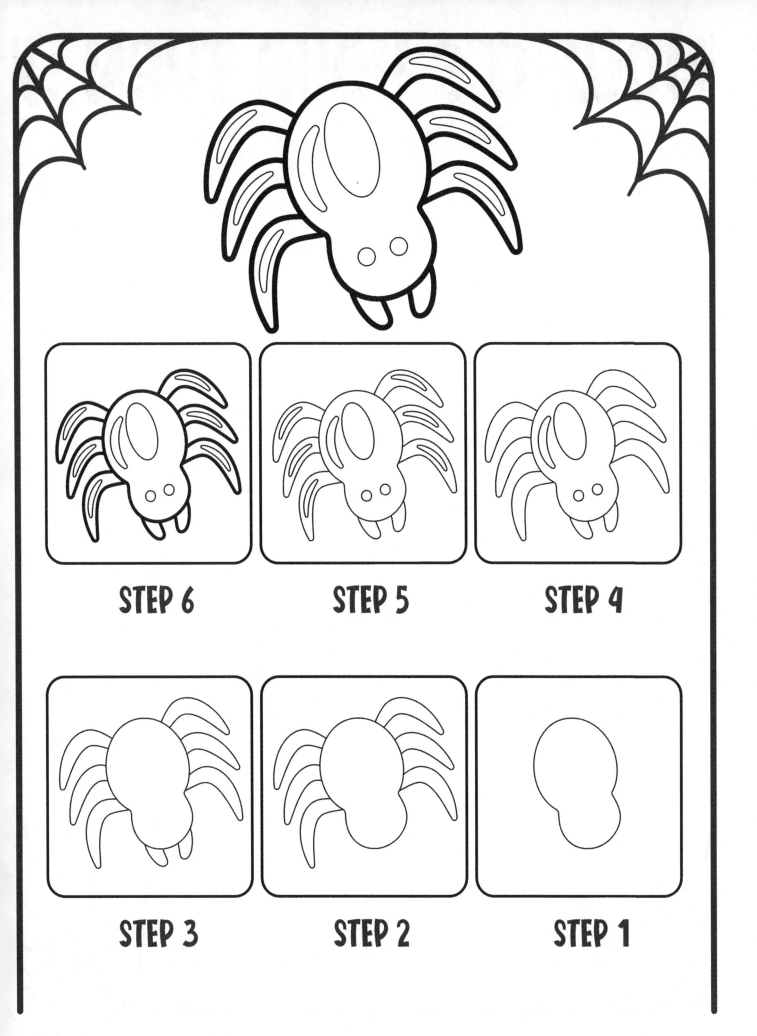

STEP 6

STEP 5

STEP 4

STEP 3

STEP 2

STEP 1

NOW, IT'S YOUR TURN :)

STEP 6

STEP 5

STEP 4

STEP 3

STEP 2

STEP 1

NOW, IT'S YOUR TURN :)

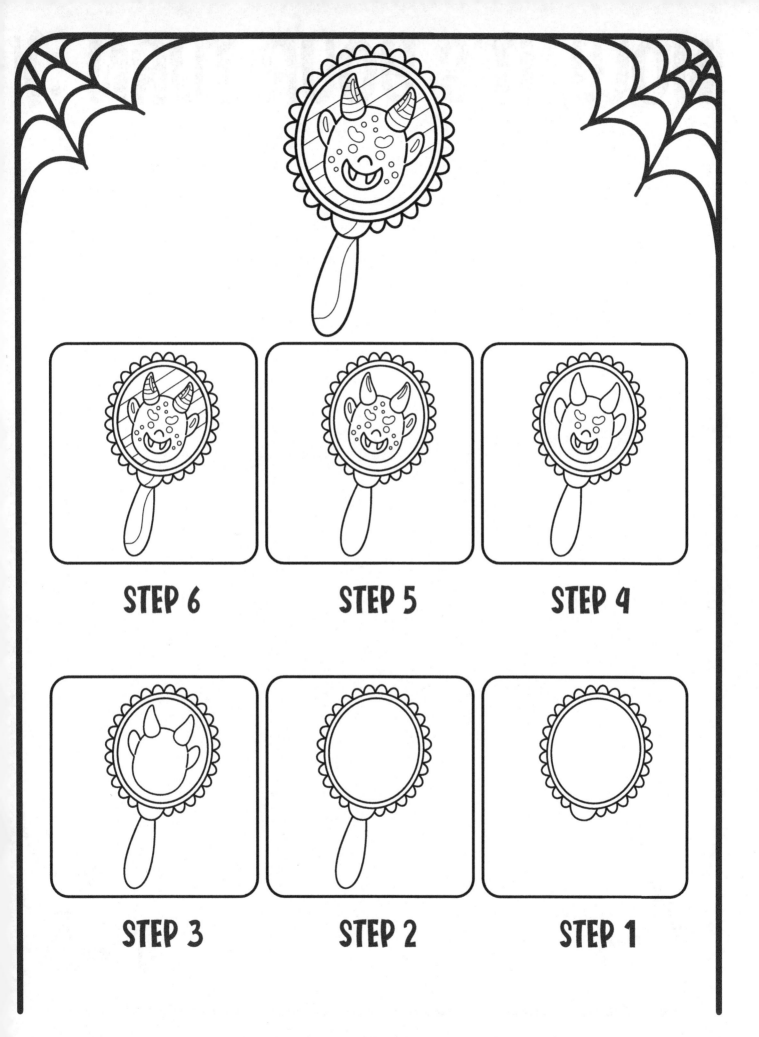

STEP 6

STEP 5

STEP 4

STEP 3

STEP 2

STEP 1

NOW, IT'S YOUR TURN :)

STEP 6

STEP 5

STEP 4

STEP 3

STEP 2

STEP 1

NOW, IT'S YOUR TURN :)

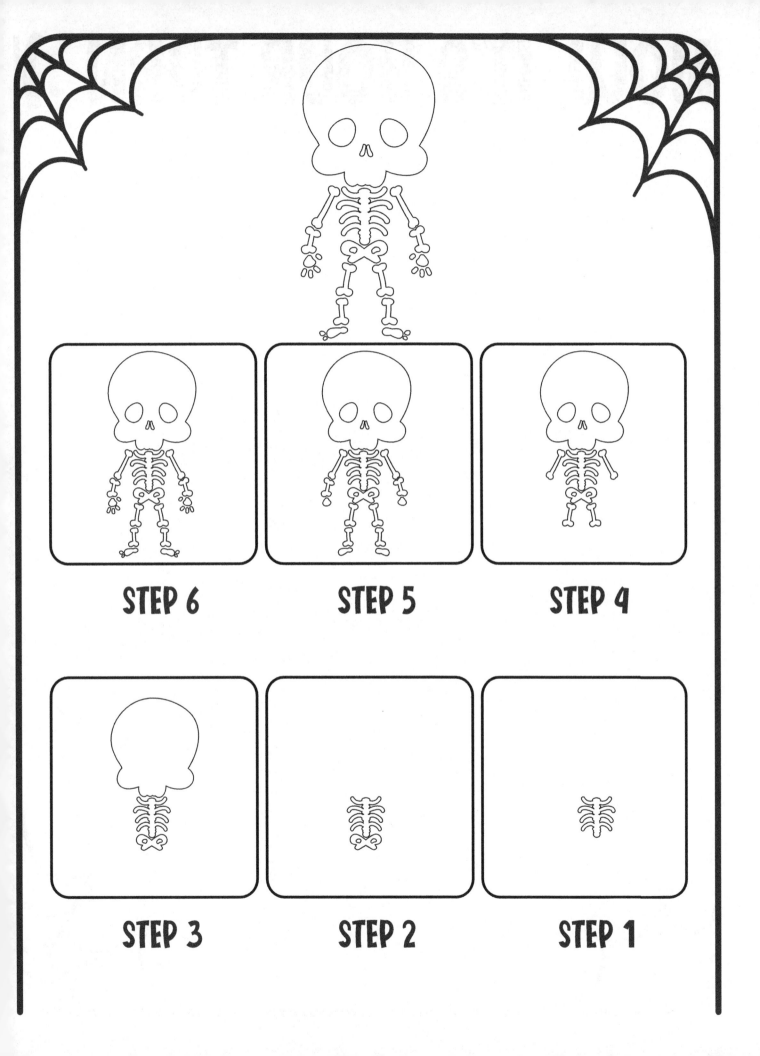

STEP 6

STEP 5

STEP 4

STEP 3

STEP 2

STEP 1

NOW, IT'S YOUR TURN :)

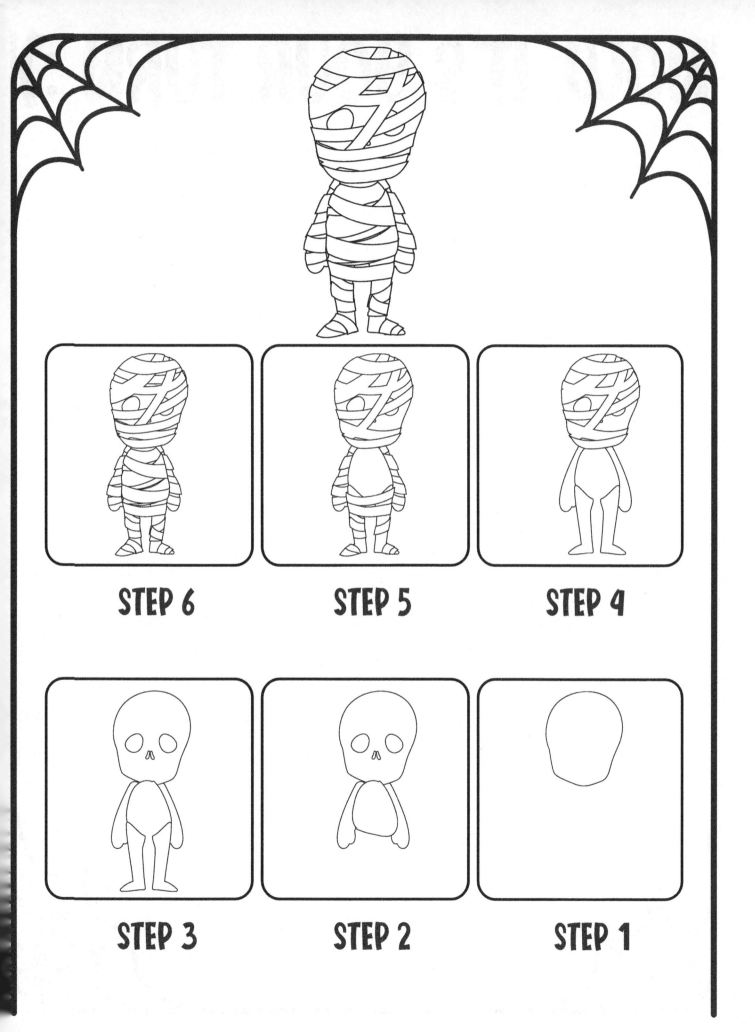

STEP 6

STEP 5

STEP 4

STEP 3

STEP 2

STEP 1

NOW, IT'S YOUR TURN :)

STEP 6

STEP 5

STEP 4

STEP 3

STEP 2

STEP 1

NOW, IT'S YOUR TURN :)

STEP 6

STEP 5

STEP 4

STEP 3

STEP 2

STEP 1

NOW, IT'S YOUR TURN :)

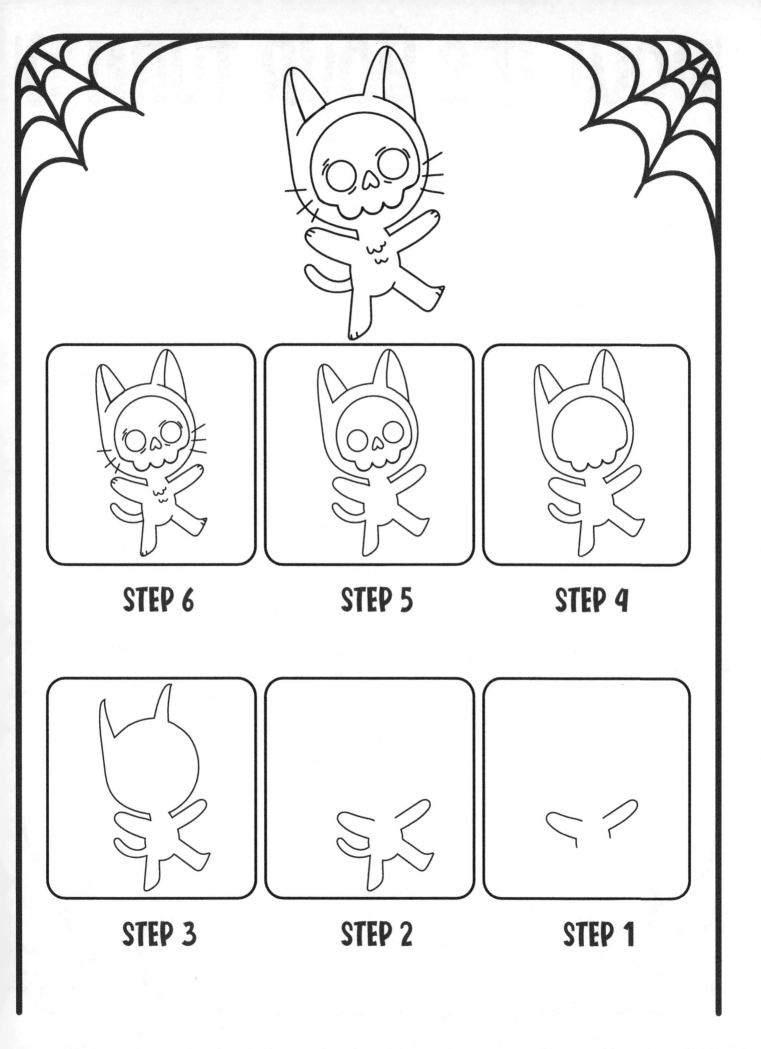

STEP 6

STEP 5

STEP 4

STEP 3

STEP 2

STEP 1

NOW, IT'S YOUR TURN :)

ENJOYING THIS BOOK? PLEASE LEAVE A REVIEW BECAUSE WE WOULD LOVE TO HEAR YOUR FEEDBACK AND ADVICE IN ORDER TO CREATE EVEN BETTER PRODUCTS FOR YOU! THANK YOU VERY MUCH FOR YOUR CHOICE! WE APPRECIATE YOU!

SEE MORE OF OUR BOOKS!

Made in the USA
Las Vegas, NV
13 December 2024

14140468R00037